Effortless Skiing

A Two-Step Technique that Makes Alpine Skiing Simple

Natalia Dounskaia

ISBN: 9798718052442

Edition 2, 2021

Acknowledgements
I am grateful to Kevin Elverum for allowing me to take his photos that are used on the cover page and in Figures 2, 6, 7, 9, 11, 12, 15.

Also, figures are used from web collections Pixabay, Unsplash, and Pexels.

I am also grateful to Dr. Astrid Klocke, Ivan Dremin, and Andrew Coulson who edited my book and to Marianna Baidoon who contributed to this book as a designer, model, and photographer.

Disclaimer
Skiing is a dangerous sport. The author disclaims any liability and responsibility resulting from the use of the information contained in this book. Any action you take upon the information in this book is strictly at your own risk.

Contents

Preface 2

Chapter I. Introduction

    I.1. What This Book is about. 3

    I.2. The Theory of Movement Control that Helps Us to Understand Skiing 6

Chapter II. Application of the Leading Joint Theory to Alpine Skiing Reveals a Two-Step Technique

    II.1. The Leading Joint during Skiing is the Upper Torso 8

    II.2. Step 1: Creating Torsion within the Body 8

    II.3. Step 2: Releasing the torsion energy to transit to the next arc 11

Chapter III. The Two-Step Technique: Outcomes, Benefits, Specific Instructions, and Helpful Drills

    III.1. Outcomes of the Two-Step Technique 16

    III.2. Advantages of the Two-Step Technique 17

    III.3. Specific Instructions on Making Turns 18

    III.4. Skiing in Special Conditions 23

    III.5. Drills 25

Conclusions 27

References 28

Preface

If you search for books on skiing, you will find at least two dozen of them. All of them are written by expert skiers. The present book is an exception from that rule. I am merely a recreational skier. I ski worse than many for whom this book is intended. However, I am a researcher who studies how the brain organizes control of complex human movements. A concept I have developed has allowed me to obtain a key understanding of the movements performed by expert skiers. My discovery shows that skiing is a simple, easy-to-learn skill. The findings of my research offer revolutionary changes in how we teach skiing. The new approach will help a wide range of skiers, from novices to experts, to radically improve their skill.

Many people may have difficulty to believe that research can provide better guidance than expert skiers. From reading books on skiing, browsing skiing Internet sites, and chatting with people on chair lifts, I have found that skillful skiers typically do not know what their body does to make a turn. Sounds incredible? Consider this then – it still remains unknown how most basic motor skills are performed. For example, it remains a mystery to scientists how we walk or even stand, keeping the body upright. It is therefore not surprising that the strategy used by the body to perform turns while skiing remains unknown. As a result, skiing instruction is often ineffective and even misleading. The purpose of this book is to cardinally change this unfortunate situation.

Whether you are a beginner or expert skier, a clear understanding how to make a turn will boost your skill level. However, I expect that this book will be most beneficial to recreational skiers who have been struggling to improve their skill for years or even decades, with little success. There are lots of people like that; I was one of them just a few years ago. This was the reason why I wanted to apply my movement control theory specifically to alpine skiing. I started to ski when I was 20 and immediately became a passionate skier. I therefore tried to do everything I could to learn to ski well. I read all the books that I could find. I spent as much time on the slopes as I could. Great skiers gave me instructions. And still, I could not catch the right movement. This struggle lasted for more than 30 years!

What a variety of instructions were given to me! I tried them all. Although they helped me to improve to some extent, the way I was making turns was still not right. While this was obvious, I did not know what I had to change to make it right. At a young age, my motor abilities helped me to compensate for the lack of skill to some extent, especially when the snow was groomed and light and the slope was not too steep. However, ice, powder, and steeper slopes would make me miserable. Later, in my fifties, I became even more dependent on good snow and usually did not dare to attempt anything steeper than a well-groomed double-blue slope. Another huge struggle that I had all those years was a crucifying pain in my leg muscles that usually started a couple of hours into skiing, not to mention that my muscles were extremely sore the next day. Who would have expected that closer to sixty, my skiing skills would skyrocket, I would start skiing black moguls, ice would stop bothering me, my legs would not get tired after spending a whole day on the slopes, and I would have no muscle soreness the next day! A two-step skiing technique that I derived from my movement control theory and that I present in this book made the trick.

Chapter I. Introduction

I.1. What this Book is about

This book is about how to make turns on parallel skis. If this is your first day on slopes, please, follow the basic steps first described elsewhere – learn how to traverse and plow. This is necessary to develop elementary stability and feeling of ski and snow dynamics. Return to this book when you are ready to start learning turns on parallel skis.

Lots of information is available these days on how to ski through books, videos, and websites. I have reviewed everything that I could find. One striking observation from this review is the huge number of various recommendations. Here are just some of them:

Load both skis equally; load predominantly the outside ski; lean forward; keep the torso facing down the hill; keep the torso quiet; keep the torso motionless; keep the arms down the hill; initiate each turn with planting the pole; initiate each turn with pushing against the back part of the skis; initiate each turn by extending the upper leg; initiate each turn with a commitment; lean the legs but keep the upper body upright; move the legs in the direction you want to go and keep the upper body calm; keep the skis flat; carve the skis...

The list can be continued. Three important observations can be gleaned from this list.

Observation 1: The number of instructions is overwhelming. The skier is supposed to focus on many things simultaneously, including arm and leg movements, the position of the upper body, direction and edging of the skis, the distribution of weight between the skis, and positioning of it along the skis. This is difficult if not impossible to do because the number of items we can simultaneously focus our attention on is very limited. During skiing, it is necessary to constantly attend to the current changes in the terrain. We can add one, probably two other items to concentrate on, but not more. All other items will go unattended until we switch our attention to them and abandon those we focused on previously. Thus, to be usable, the instructions need to be very simple. Optimally, they need to highlight just one single aspect of the movement. Two aspects can also be practiced but only if they need to be attended sequentially, not simultaneously. As you will see later, the two-step technique I offer satisfies this simplicity requirement, including only <u>two dominant elements that are performed sequentially</u>. These two key elements create a foundation for skiing in all conditions. As soon as these elements have been acquired, the skill can be further refined through focusing on some minor points.

Observation 2: Ski instructors cannot explain clearly, why the suggested actions need to be done. For example, one of the most frequently given instructions is to keep the shoulders "facing downhill" (or "quiet" or "motionless"). Have you tried to ask why? If you have, the answer was probably something like "this is the way how we ski". The inability to explain why suggested actions need to be performed shows that there is no clear understanding of skiing biomechanics currently available. My research enabled me to figure out skiing biomechanics. According to it, we do not need to care about facing downhill or keeping the shoulders motionless. This will happen by itself as <u>a natural consequence</u> of the actions that I suggest performing, and that each good skier performs, usually without realizing this. Another frequently given instruction is to keep the body forward so that the pressure on the skis would be applied in front of the boots, not behind the boots. While this indeed needs to be done, instructors do not explain how to achieve this. My interpretation suggests that there are two time points during a turn when we need to push the body's center of mass forward, and we do it in a specific way at each of the two points.

Figure 1. Gravity resists transitions. The skier is at the end of a turn to his right, and he is prepared to transit to a turn to his left. The center of mass of the body, which is at about the belt height, is to his right from the skis and close to the ground. The yellow arrow represents gravitational force that pulls down his center of mass and keeps it to his right from the skis. The red arrow shows the force that would apply to the center of mass if the skier extends the inner leg. This force would pull the center of mass further away from the skis. To transit to the next turn, there are no muscles that could overcome gravity and pull or push his center of mass directly to the other side of the skis from this position.

Observation 3: The instructions provide little information on how to initiate a turn. The instructions on how to ski usually tell us what to do before we initiate a turn, and after we have entered the turn, with little explanations on *how to initiate the turn*. I was able to find only a few suggestions on how to initiate a turn. Let us consider each of them.

Hopping. Many years ago, when I started to ski, the major idea was that turns are made by hopping. Although skiers usually did not hop, the explanation was largely accepted, simply because there was no better explanation. Now, skis have become more carved, resulting in smoother skiing. It has therefore become apparent that we do not hop to make a turn. New ideas have emerged that can be classified in two groups, steering and transitions.

Steering. The steering idea suggests that at the end of the previous turn, we need to steer the tips of the skis to the direction to which we want to go next. It is implied, and often explicitly expressed, that the change of the direction is done by the legs. It is less clear what parts of the legs should be used and how, but some instructions suggest that the change of the ski direction is done by rotating the legs in the hip sockets.

Transitions. This approach tells us to initiate a turn by shifting the body's center of mass from one side of the skis to the other. Some instructors say that we do it by extending the inner leg. This approach is not alternative to steering because it can be suggested that both are being done simultaneously.

I think skiers do none of the above. It is true that the legs get rotated in the hip sockets and the center of mass gets shifted to the other side of the skis, but not as a result of a direct and intended action, but <u>*as a consequence*</u> of some other actions. One problem associated with the recommendations included in both steering and transitions is that the suggested actions are physically impossible. Indeed, observe the skier in Figure 1. He is just preparing to initiate a turn to his left. We can see that his center of mass is very low, near the ground, and that the gravitational force points well away from the skis. <u>There are no muscles in the body that can pull the center of mass laterally, from this position to the other side of the skis</u>. *<u>Since the center of mass is to the side of the skis, we also have no leverage to push against the ground to shift the center of mass over to the other side.</u>* If the skier extends the inner leg, the generated force (shown in the Figure with the red arrow) will push the body's center of mass further away from the skis.

Figure 2. Lifting the body during a transition. The skier has finished the turn to his right and is fully prepared to initiate the turn to his left in posture 1. The transition of the center of mass over the skis is made through postures 2-5. Through these four postures, he gradually straightens the legs, and therefore, the center of mass is lifted up higher than it was before the turn in posture 1.

Furthermore, the center of mass of the body usually lifts up during its transition over the skis. This can be seen in Figure 2. The skier in this figure is fully prepared to initiate his next turn in frame 1. The transition of the center of mass over the skis is made through frames 2-5. Through these frames, the skier gradually straightens the legs, and therefore, the center of mass is lifted higher than it was in frame 1. Neither the steering nor transition interpretation can explain what forces lift the center of mass and move it over the skis.

While we cannot move the center of mass laterally in the position shown in Figure 1 and in posture 1 of Figure 2, we can move it forward. We therefore shift it to the other side from the skis along an inverted U-shape trajectory (∩). But we do not do it intentionally. Rather, the center of mass moves along the ∩–trajectory as a result of the two actions that we perform consecutively, as I will describe in Chapter II.

Before I move on to the descriptions of the two key actions, I need to first make two comments.

First, when you start reading these descriptions, you must *forget all the instructions you previously learned*. The biomechanical model of skiing I used to determine the two key actions is unique, and therefore, my instructions differ from the majority of the instructions that I have heard of.

Second, my interpretation of the skiing technique is *counterintuitive*. It contradicts what our eyes tell us. While going up a mountain on a chair lift, I often talk about my interpretation with skiers sitting next to me. I have found that it is difficult for people to accept my interpretation, and the resistance is proportional to the skier's skill level. Therefore, before I present my interpretation, I need to describe a physical phenomenon that explains why and how my two-step technique works.

I.2. The Theory of Movement Control that Helps Us to Understand Skiing

Basically, all movements that we perform involve rotations of more than a single joint. In motor control research, we say that movements are multi-joint. Each joint is spanned by several muscles some of which pull the joint into flexion and the others into extension. However, activity of the muscles is not always necessary for the joint to rotate because it can rotate passively due to motion of another joint of the limb. This is like when we move the handle of a whip, the whole whip comes in motion in coordination with the handle movement. You can test this passive motion with a simple experiment. Relax the wrist muscles and repetitively flex and extend the elbow, as the girl does in Figure 3. If you perform the movement fast, the relaxed wrist will rotate, and the hand will flop up and down passively, by inertia. To prevent this passive motion and keep the hand aligned with the forearm, wrist muscles need to counteract the inertial forces. The same happens during all other movements of our limbs: rotation at one joint mechanically affects the other limb's joints. Therefore, by activating the muscles at one joint, we can bring to motion our other joints, without activating their local groups of muscles.

<u>Figure 3.</u> **Active elbow rotation causes passive wrist rotation.** If we repetitively flex and extend the elbow while keeping the wrist muscles relaxed, the wrist rotates and the hand flops up and down passively, by inertia. Similarly, motion at a single joint causes passive forces at the other joints during all body movements.

Note that another person watching your elbow and wrist movement may think that you are producing motion of both joints actively, using muscles at each joint. In other cases, it is possible that a seemingly motionless joint generates energy for the entire movement. An example is puddling a kayak. When we look at a skillful kayaker, we see that his torso is quiet, and the arms rotate and move the puddle. However, it is well known that skillful kayakers use the core muscles to rotate the trunk around its longitudinal axis (a movement that is hardly noticeable) while the arms transmit the energy generated by the trunk to the paddle.

These examples show that when we observe a multi-joint movement, it is often hard to say which muscles at which joints cause it. In particular, if the legs rotate in the hip sockets during skiing, this does not necessarily mean that we actively perform this rotation. *The hip rotation may be a result of passive effects of motion from the other parts of the body*. If the torso looks motionless, it is still possible that the core muscles rotate it with respect to the legs, generating energy for ski turns. In addition to the mechanical effect of motion of the body parts on each other (in movement control research we call this mechanical effect "inter-segmental dynamics"), two other mechanical factors influence rotation of our joints during skiing, gravity and the interaction of the skis with the slope.

My theory of human movement control provides an interpretation of how the mechanical factors affecting a motor action are used by the brain for movement production.[1] The most essential idea in this theory is that a single joint is used to generate energy for the entire multi-joint movement. This joint is termed the **leading** join. The leading joint is rotated actively, by the muscles spanning it, and it generates passive mechanical forces at the other joints that are termed **trailing** joints. In the experiment you have performed (Figure 3), the elbow was the leading joint and the wrist was the trailing joint. The wrist musculature can modify the passive motion at this joint depending on the task that needs to be performed, for example, if we want to fix the wrist and keep the hand aligned with the forearm. This theory suggests that during skiing, as during other multi-joint movements, there is a single joint in the body that plays the leading role in the performance of the entire movement. Motion at this joint generates energy for the turns, bringing the other joints to motion passively. Surely, as soon as I figured out the leading joint, or rather the leading body segment, the entire organization of downhill skiing became transparent.

---

[1] If you are interested to know more about the theory, a summary paper (Dounskaia 2010) presents it in a simplified way.

Chapter II. Application of the Leading Joint Theory to Alpine Skiing Reveals a Two-Step Technique

II.1. The Leading Segment during Skiing is the Upper Torso

Next, I am going to convince you that *we make skiing turns by rotating the upper torso with respect to the lower body*.

I know, this is not what ski instructors tell you. And I know this is hard to believe because when we look at a good skier we see that their torso is nearly motionless. It is indeed motionless with respect to the environment (the fall-line, hills, trees, and observers). However, it rotates relative to the lower body. *When the skis turn, we rotate the torso in the opposite direction. As a result, the torso looks motionless to an observer*. However, this look is deceptive because the core muscles work vehemently to rotate the upper body relative to the lower body. So, the "motionless" and "quiet" torso is an illusion!

The torso rotation is the first step of what I call *a two-step technique*. The torso rotation plays the leading role because during this step, we generate energy within the body that we use during the second step to move our legs. Thus, a turn is performed in *two consecutive steps*. Step 1 is a creation of torsion within the body through rotation of the torso away from the direction in which the skis go (counter rotation). Step 2 is a release of this torsion and usage of it for transition of the skis. Let us consider each step in more detail.

II.2. Step 1: Creating Torsion within the Body

Creating torsion within a bar means twisting it as shown in Figure 4. Step 1 is to do something similar with our body. Figure 5 shows a skier at the points where he has generated torsion of the body and is prepared to initiate step 2. At each of these points, the skier is at the end of the corresponding arc. Therefore, we create torsion while going through the arc, and, more precisely, during the second half of the arc.

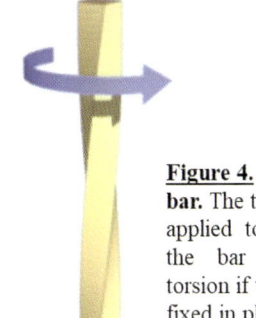

Figure 4. Torsion of a bar. The twisting force applied to the top of the bar can create torsion if the bottom is fixed in place.

How do we generate the torsion? Let us look again at the bar in Figure 4. The bar torsion can be generated if we twist its top as the arrow shows. If the bar is not fixed at the bottom, the twisting force will rotate the bar as a whole and no torsion will emerge. Torsion will be created if the bottom of the bar is either fixated or rotated in the opposite direction. When the skis go through an arc, they rotate because they are carving a turn. They are of course also *locked in the snow*, and more so because the skis are edged (tilted up the slope, which creates an angle between the skis and slope). We therefore can create torsion within the body by rotating the shoulders in the direction opposite to that in which the skis are rotating. This is what the skier in Figure 5 does. At the end of arc 1, the skis are rotating to the skier's left and the shoulders are rotated to the right. Subsequently during the next turn, the skis go to the skier's right and the shoulders are rotated to the left at the end of arc 2.

Figure 6 provides a clearer picture of a skier who just created torsion in his body. The skis of this skier are finishing the arc to his right and his shoulders are rotated in the opposite direction. The skis rotate to the right due to edging and sidecut. They are locked in the snow. Like with twisting the bar with the locked bottom, the skier creates torsion in the body by rotating his upper torso to the left. Thus, the major action that the skier performs at this moment is the torso rotation to the left using his core muscles, while the skis rotate to the right mechanically, "pulling" the legs in the same direction.

There are several tricks that we use to further increase the torsion in the body. The main one is that we do not rotate the shoulders around the longitudinal axis of the torso, like the bar in Figure 4 is rotated. Instead, we use our body's additional flexibility to increase torsion: we rotate the shoulders at a downwards angle to the longitudinal axis of the torso. This is done by pulling the outside shoulder downward during the rotation of the torso. For example, the skier in Figures 6 and 7 rotates the upper torso to his left and simultaneously pulls his left (outside) shoulder down. This is depicted by the red arrow at the outside shoulder in Figure 7. To allow the shoulder to move down, the skier bends the body laterally to his left.

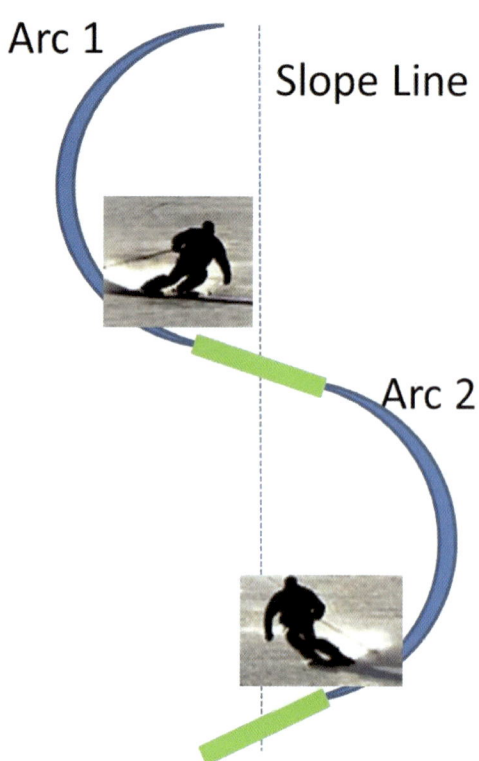

Figure 5. **Body torsion is generated right before a transition.** At the end of each arc, the skier creates torsion within the body by rotating the shoulders in the direction opposite to that in which the skis turn. The green bars show transitions between the arcs.

Figure 8 shows another example of the posture achieved through the slanted shoulder rotation. While the skis point to the skier's left, the shoulders are rotated to his right. Also, the skier is pulling the right shoulder down, and the body is giving in to this pull by bending right. Figure 9 shows the same posture from the back.

It is not apparent from Figures 6 - 9 that the skiers are pulling the outer shoulder down because both shoulders are positioned at the same horizontal level. The shoulders are horizontal because the entire body is inclined inside the arc. If you try to perform this slanted shoulder rotation to your right while standing on the floor, you will see that the bending of the body to the right positions the right shoulder lower in comparison with the left shoulder.

The body bending is produced through the following changes in the body posture:

1. Flexing of the hip on the outer side of the turn towards the inside of the turn (indicated in Figures 7, 8, 9 by the green arrows) and accordingly jutting out the inner hip.

2. Flexing of both knees.

3. Pushing the outer knee inside the arc behind the inner knee. The yellow arrow indicates this action in Figures 7, 8, 9. For this purpose, the skiers have the outside ski slightly lagging the inside ski. This allows the skiers to push the outside knee inside the arc behind the inside knee.

Figure 6. Counter rotation of the torso with respect to the lower body. At this moment, the skis finish going on the arc to the skier's right. The counter rotation of the shoulders to the skier's left causes torsion within the body. The red arrows emphasize the opposite directions of rotation of the skis and shoulders.

Figure 7. Body movements that increase torsion. To increase torsion in preparation to initiate the turn to the left, the skier, while rotating the shoulders to his left, also pulls the left shoulder down, as shown by the red arrow. To give in to the slanted shoulder rotation, the skier bends the body to his left as shown by the green arrow. The bending causes jutting of the right hip out. The bending also causes the skis to edge, as the blue arrow shows. To increase torsion even further, the skier pushes the outside (left) knee inside of the turn (to the right), behind the inside (right) knee, as shown by the yellow arrow.

These three actions allow the skiers to increase rotation of the upper torso away from the direction of the skis, and thus, increase torsion of the body. Instructors often formulate jutting out of the inside hip and lateral flexion of the outside knee as separate goals that a skier needs to focus on. Also, the rotation of the shoulders and lateral bending of the torso are often presented as two separate actions, "counter rotation" and "angulation", respectively. According to my interpretation, none of the three actions has an independent value. *All three of them are secondary actions* that support the development of torsion within the body by *allowing the upper torso to increase its counter rotation*. All three become a single action if we rotate the upper torso with a twist of the outside shoulder downward and *allowing the rest of the body to give in to this "slanted shoulder rotation"*. Then the body bending at the hips (angulation) and knee flexing happen naturally. Pushing the outside knee inside the arc behind the inside knee is a trick that requires an additional cognitive effort during learning. We therefore should consider it as an action that refines the technique and postpone practicing it until after we have learned to perform the other movement.

Figure 8. **Slanted shoulder rotation at the end of a turn to the left.** The skier has accumulated torsion in the body at the end of the turn. While the skis point to his left, the shoulders are counter-rotated to the right. The skier pulls the right shoulder down, as shown by the red arrow. This results in the body bending right at the right hip, as shown by the green arrow. Accordingly, the left hip sticks out. The body bend to the right is further increased by pushing the right knee to the left at the rear of the left leg, as shown by the yellow arrow.

Figure 9. **A view of the slanted shoulder rotation from the back at the end of a turn to the left.** The torsion accumulated in the body through the counter rotation of the shoulders is indicated by the diagonal folds on the top of the skier's jacket. The body bends to the right because the skier pulls the right shoulder down. The arrows of the same colors as in Figure 7 indicate the pulling the right shoulder down (red), bending of the body to the right (green), and pushing the right knee to the left (yellow).

There are several important consequences of and advantages to the torsion generated at the end of each arc. We will discuss them in detail below in Chapter III. Now, let us move on to step 2 of the two-step technique and consider how the torsion is used to transit to the next arc.

II.3. Step 2: Releasing the Torsion Energy to Transit to the Next Arc

Creating the torsion of the body in step 1 prepares us for step 2 in which we release the torsion energy and use it to transit to the next arc. Let us again consider the twisted position of the body at the end of arc 1 in Figure 5. In this position, the skier's shoulders are rotated to his right and the skis are rotated to his left. The body can forcibly stay in this twisted position while the skis are locked in the snow and the skier uses the core muscles to rotate the shoulders. If he relaxes the core muscles at this moment, the torsion energy will release by rotating his shoulders to his left and aligning the upper body with the lower body. But this would leave the skis still continuing their leftwards turn – and it is time to initiate the next turn to the right! So the other way to release the torsion energy, and help start the next turn, is to unlock the skis from the snow. If the friction between the skis and snow disappears, or becomes sufficiently small, the torsion energy can release by rotating the skis to the skier's right, thus re-aligning the lower body with the upper body. This would change the direction in which the skis go. That is exactly what we do. Now let us consider how it is achieved.

We do *not* hop to unlock the skis from the snow. Instead, we shift the body's weight by "throwing" the belly/pelvis down the hill, which is the direction that our counter-rotated shoulders are facing at this moment. A helpful landmark to which we can push the pelvis is the tip of the outer ski because at this moment, it is located right in front of our counter-rotated shoulders. This shift of the body weight forward has two consequences. First, the body weight moves from inside of the arc downhill, and thus, towards the skis which are at an angle to the slope line at this moment. This eliminates the ski's edging, and thus, unlocks the skis from the snow. Second, the shift forward also unloads the back parts of the skis, reducing their friction with the snow. As a result, *the torsion within our body releases via pivoting the flat skis around the tips.* The skis pivot under the body from one side of it to the other, and therefore, they start to point in the new direction. This change of the ski direction is effortless because the leg muscles work only to push the body weight forward. The rotation of the legs in the hip sockets involved in the pivoting of the skis under the body is done passively, by the released torsion.

You can experience the rotating effect of the torsion release while standing on the floor. It will be better if the floor surface has low friction (tile or laminate would be better than carpet). Even better, do this exercise in ski boots because of their firm footing. Create the torsion so that after you have turned the shoulders, you are facing a sofa, or a table, and your feet are under acute angle with (or almost parallel to) the sofa/table edge. In this twisted position, lean forward, toward the sofa, with the entire body. Support yourself with the arms against the sofa to prevent falling. The lean should not be achieved by bending the upper body at the hips. The whole body should lean toward the sofa as a rigid bar, with your pelvis leading the lean. If you do this, your heels will detach from the floor and your boots will stand on the tips. You will see that as soon as you detach the heels from the ground, the boots will pivot around the tips and align with your torso, facing the sofa. The torsion within the body will disappear because the removal of the friction has allowed the torsion energy to rotate and re-align your lower body.

When we are on our skis, the moving of the pelvis forward can be achieved in two ways. The most energetic way, which is usually used, is to push against the ground with our legs through extension of the knees and hips. The second way is to make the same movement more gently, with minimal extension of the body, mainly by pushing against the ground with the feet and ankles within the boots. Then the knees and hips will remain flexed. This technique was suggested by Harald Harb (2006). The first way is however more effective and easier to perform, and I therefore recommend using it, at least at the beginning of practice.

Let us look how the skier in Figure 10 performs step 2. Frame 1 is the posture shown at the end of arc 1 in Figure 5. Torsion is maximal in this position, and the skier is ready to initiate step 2. The skier is pushing the pelvis forward by extending the hips and knees in frame 2. This eliminates edging and breaks the back part of the skis free from the snow, which allows the body torsion to release and pivot the skis around their front tips. Frame 3 shows the skier in the middle of the pivoting motion of the skis. In this frame, the body is extended even more than in frame 2. The skier's posture looks unstable because the skis have little grip with the ground, and the body is largely "flying" in the air. In frame 4, the skis have already pivoted to the other side of the body, and the skier starts to load the skis by landing on them. In fact, the skier lands on the inner side of the skis, and therefore, the skis edge. He does this because he already starts slanting (pulling down) the outer shoulder, which is seen as the angle between the upper and lower body (body angulation). Due to the edging, the skis lock in the snow and start carving the next arc. The skier continues to load the skis and slant the shoulder in frame 5. The skier starts to rotate the slanted shoulders to accumulate torsion within the body at the apex of the arc (frame 6). In frame 7, the skier continues this torso motion by rotating the shoulders further to his left and supporting this motion by bending the body via jutting out of the inner hip and flexing of the knees. This action continues into frame 8. In this posture, maximal body torsion is accumulated. Next, the skier pushes the body weight forward by extending the knees and hips, with the pelvis leading this motion (frame 9). This initiates the transition to the next arc.

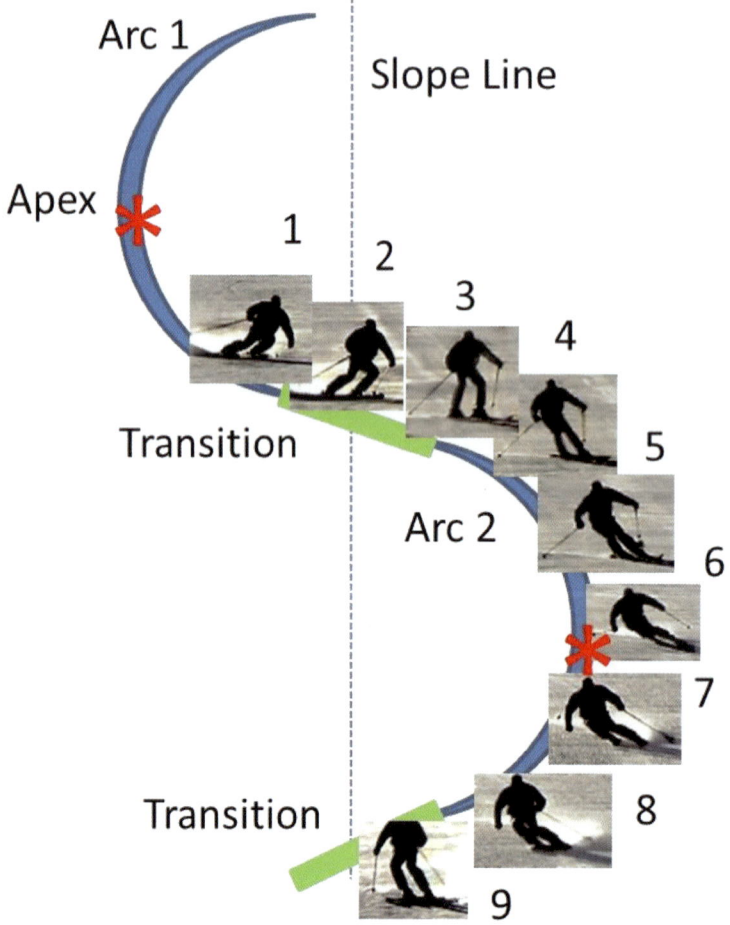

Figure 10. Transition from arc 1 to arc 2 and posture changes through arc 2. The arcs are shown with the blue color. The green lines show the transitions to the next arc. The red star marks the apex of each arc, i.e., the point where the skis are directed downhill.

Consider another example of transitioning to the next arc shown in Figure 2 which is copied here as Figure 11. Frame 1 shows the skier at the end of the previous arc. The skis are to the left from the skier's body weight, pointing to his right, and the shoulders are rotated left, causing torsion in the body. The skier is gradually pushing the body forward in frames 2 and 3. This movement flattens the skis and breaks the back parts of the skis free from the ground, allowing the torsion to pivot the skis around their front tips. Frame 4 shows the skier in the middle of the pivoting motion of the skis. In frame 5, the skis have transited to the right side of the skier, and he starts to load the skis with his weight and edge them by pulling his right shoulder down. This locks the skis in the new arc. The skis are starting to move left from the fall-line and the skier starts to rotate his slanted shoulders to the right in frame 6.

Figure 11. Consecutive postures of a skier during a transition to the next turn. The skier has finished the turn to his right and developed body torsion in frame 1. He started pushing his center of mass forward in frame 2 and continued to do this in frame 3. As a result, the skis broke free from the friction with the ground. This released the body torsion that caused pivoting of the skis under the skier's body (frame 4). The skis pivoted to the other side of the skier's body (frame 5). This completed the transition to the new arc, and the skier started to load the skis to carve around this arc.

To summarize, the technique for alpine skiing turns described above includes two steps. The first step can be considered preparatory. While the skis are locked in the snow, going through the current arc, the skier _accumulates torsion energy_ by rotating the upper body with respect to the lower body, using his core muscles. The second step is _releasing the torsion energy to change the direction of the skis_ and transiting them to the other side of the skier. To achieve this, the skier inclines the entire body forward by pushing the feet against the ground and extending the knees and hips. This flattens the skis and breaks the back portions of the skis free from friction with the ground, allowing the torsion energy to work and pivot the skis under the skier around their front tips. Thus, _we use our muscles to generate torsion within our body (our core muscles accomplish that) while the legs passively transit the skis to the other side of the body, due to the released torsion energy_. We should provide minimal resistance to this ski motion. It can be observed in Figure 12 that active effort produced by the skiers during the transitions is minimal. This figure shows examples of skier's postures in the middle of the transition from one arc to another. All skiers are almost flying above their skis while the skis are pivoting from one side of the skier to the other.

A typical mistake that prevents proper performance of the two-step technique is bending the torso forward. Crouching is harmful for both steps. In step 1, crouching will decrease our ability to generate torsion. In step 2, crouching will resist the shift of the body weight forward. So, it is important to keep the torso upright through the entire turn.

The two-step technique increases the skier's stability by providing a strong grip of the skis with the snow, even on icy slopes, and requires minimal effort from the skier, so the leg muscles do not get tired. Also, _many movement elements emphasized by ski instructors emerge as side effects of the two-step technique_. These and some other points that refine the use of this technique, including the maintenance of the body weight in the forward position, are discussed in detail in the next chapter.

Figure 12. Postures of expert skiers in the middle of a transition between consecutive arcs. The skiers are shown at the moment when the skis pivot around their tips from one side of the skier to the other. The postures look unstable because the grip of the skis with the snow is low, and the body almost "flies" above the skis.

Chapter III. The Two-Step Technique: Outcomes, Benefits, Specific Instructions, and Helpful Drills

III.1. Outcomes of the Two-Step Technique

Facing downhill. Keeping the shoulders facing downhill is probably the #1 instruction provided by ski instructors. It is also often formulated as "keeping the torso still" or "motionless" or "separated" from the lower body. This movement feature however naturally happens as a side effect of step 1, i.e., generation of torsion within the body. Indeed, when a skier is at the apex of an arc, the skis point downhill and both the upper and lower body face the same direction as well. After the skier passes the apex, the skis start to turn away from the fall-line. To generate torsion, the skier at the same time starts to rotate the shoulders in the opposite direction. Because of this counter rotation of the skis and shoulders, the shoulders remain facing downhill. *For an external observer, the torso of the skier looks motionless*, even though the core muscles are working hard to rotate the upper body with respect to the lower body. This misleading observation causes a conclusion that, to ski well, we need to keep the torso motionless, facing downhill. Although the seemingly motionless torso is indeed a feature of skillful skiing, this feature should not be our goal. We cannot effectively 'command' our torso to 'remain motionless'. The seemingly motionless torso is a secondary feature that emerges as an outcome of the torsion generation.

Leg movement during between-arc transitions. When we observe a good skier, we see that the legs apparently rotate at the hips right or left with respect to the torso. A change of the angle between the legs and torso is, for example, clearly apparent in Figure 11. In postures 1-3, the skier's legs are rotated to the left with respect to his torso. The legs start to rotate to the right in posture 6. Thus, the leg rotation in the hips between left and right happens during the transition of the skis from one side to the other. However, we do not perform this leg rotation actively, as ski instructions sometimes suggest. This motion is predominantly passive, being caused by the released body torsion that untwists the body, and thus, pivots the skis around their tips. At this phase of a turn, we should try to relax our leg muscles to let our legs to give in to the released torsion, and not resist it. The slanted shoulder rotation initiated at the end of the transition period further increases the angle between the legs and torso.

Ski edging. Another element that naturally results from the correct rotation of the shoulders is ski edging. Pulling the outer shoulder down during step 1 causes the skis to edge. If you perform the slanted rotation of the shoulders while standing on the floor, you will see that in this position, you tend to edge your feet. This happens because pulling the outer shoulder down causes the hip on the inward side of the turn to jut (body angulation). During skiing, this hip motion towards the slope naturally results in ski edging against the slope. Therefore, ski edging, which is usually emphasized by instructors as a separate goal on which we need to concentrate our attention, also emerges as an outcome of the slanted shoulder rotation. This edging combined with the carved sidecut of the skis make us move along the arc.

Ski loading. Loading the outer ski more than the inner ski while going through an arc is emphasized by many instructors as a separate movement feature that needs to be practiced. But like ski edging, *loading the outer ski is a direct result of the slanted shoulder rotation* performed in step 1. We do not need to pay our attention to ski loading. It will be automatically right if we use the two-step technique.

III.2. Advantages of the Two-Step Technique

Skiing with the two-step technique has multiple advantages. Let us consider the major ones of them.

Simplicity of the technique. People whom I taught the two-step technique often related to me in surprise: "But it is so simple!". Yes, it is simple, and that is the most obvious advantage of the two-step technique. *At each moment of time, we need to focus on only one single action, first on the generation of torsion within the body and then on shifting the pelvis forward.* We do not need to worry about other elements of movement, like how we move the legs, how we load each ski, and all the other actions often recommended by instructors.

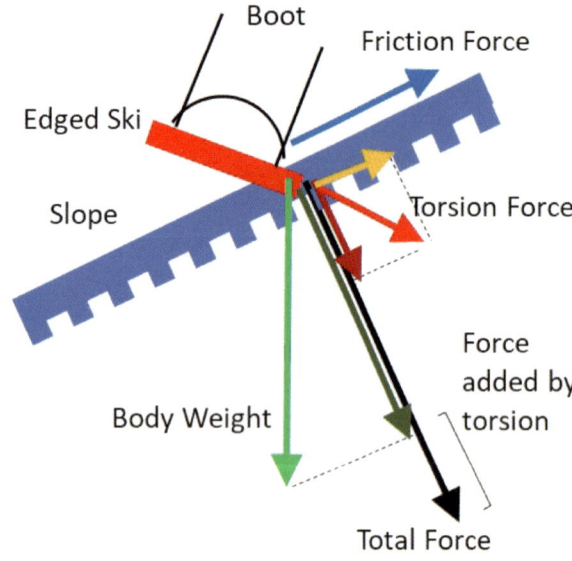

Figure 13. **Torsion increases the grip of the ski on the slope.** Forces exerted by the edged ski on the slope are shown in the frontal plane. The red bar shows the frontal projection of the ski with a boot on it. The blue bar shows the slope. The force caused by the torsion (red vector) has two components, each of which helps to prevent slipping of the ski down the slope. The first component (yellow vector) directly pushes the ski up the slope. The second component (dark red vector) increases the friction force (blue vector) between the ski and ground. This is because friction force is proportional to the total force (black vector) applied by the ski perpendicularly to the slope. While the major contributor to the total force is the body weight component (dark green vector), the torsion force also adds a component (dark red vector), thus increasing friction.

Skiing safety and stability. Another important advantage of the two-step technique is that *the body torsion caused by the slanted shoulder rotation increases the grip of the skis on the snow, providing stability even on icy slopes*. Figure 13 helps us to understand this physical effect. The red bar shows an edged ski viewed from its front and the blue bar shows the slope. The ski exerts two forces on the slope, body weight (the green vector) and a force caused by the body torsion (the red vector) that cuts the ski into the slope. Each force has a component perpendicular to the slope (the dark green and dark red vector, respectively). The sum of these two components is the total force (the black vector). Since per physics "every action has an equal and opposite reaction", the slope exerts a reaction force that causes large force of friction to the ski (the blue vector) that is proportional to the total force. Thus, the higher the total force is, the higher the friction force is that resists slipping, and the more stable our skis are. While the major contributor to the total force is the body weight, the torsion force increases the total force, and thus, the friction force. Furthermore, the other component of the torsion force (the yellow vector) directly pushes the ski up the slope. Together, both components of the torsion force add to resistance to skidding of the ski sideways, and thus, improve the grip of the ski on the slope.

Effortless turns. When you apply the two-step technique, skiing becomes effortless. Most of the muscle effort we make is for generating torsion, which comes from the use of our core muscles. *The legs should be maximally compliant to the effect of the shoulder rotation*. We should use the leg muscles for buffering the impact of the skis with the ground and not for moving the skis along and between the arcs. A clear sign that you have learned to use the torsion energy to pivot the skis is that *your thigh muscles stop hurting*. Before I started to use the two-step technique, crucifying pain emerged in my thigh muscles after mere two hours of skiing. I could hardly walk the next day because of the muscle pain. Now my legs do not get tired after a whole day of extensive skiing, and do not get sore on the following day. If you let your core muscles do the work, not only will you feel the difference, but your friends will note that your skiing looks effortless.

Conscious control of performance. Another advantage of the two-step technique is that the skier *consciously comprehends the mechanical effect* used by the body to make turns. Also, the skier has apparent feedback information about the quality of his/her turns. For example, we feel the jutting sensation in the hips, and we see the extent to which we rotated the shoulders with respect to the skis at the end of step 1 (are the skis and shoulders almost parallel?). Both allow the skier to critically assess the quality of the turns and decide what needs to be improved. *Consciously implementing the two-step technique is important.* I have noticed that when I am not fully focused on my performance of the technique, my skiing immediately deteriorates. Mental concentration on each of the two steps pays back.

One technique for all conditions. Finally, the remarkable advantage of the two-step technique is that it works in different circumstances and on all slopes. We have already discussed that the technique increases stability during skiing (see "Skiing safety and stability" in this section), which helps us to maximize friction between the skis and the snow, and thus helps us ski on icy slopes. At the end of this chapter, I will discuss how we use this technique to ski on steep slopes, on moguls, and in deep snow.

III.3. Specific Instructions on Making Turns

When you practice the two-step technique, start by solely focusing on step 1, and when you have learned it, add step 2. It is important to start practicing the two steps on mild slopes. Relatively low speed will help the skier to concentrate on the generation of torsion in step 1 without fear of losing control of their skis. Also, it can be much scarier to push the body weight forward in step 2 on steeper slopes. It is therefore important to increase the slope steepness only after the skier has mastered fluent performance of the two steps on milder slopes.

While the two steps required to make a turn are described in Chapter II, here I provide additional instructions that further specify the execution of each step. I also discuss how to keep the body weight forward and how to use the poles during the two steps.

Step 1. Generating Torsion. As we already know, to make a turn, we need to accumulate the body torsion at the end of each arc. We do it through slanted rotation of the shoulders with respect to the lower body. So, <u>*when do we need to initiate the slanted shoulder rotation?*</u> Let us again look at Figures 10 and 11. We can see that the skiers shown there land on skis that have gone past "flat" and are already edged (frame 4 of Figure 10 and frame 5 of Figure 11). They do it by pulling the outer shoulder down already at the very beginning of the arc. This causes body angulation and also the ski edging, both of which become more apparent in the next frames, i.e., frame 5 of Figure 10 and frame 6 of Figure 11. Thus, we start to pull the outer shoulder down already at the beginning of the arc. We smoothly and continuously build the shoulder counter rotation as the skis pass the arc's apex, i.e., the point where the skis are directed along the fall-line.

Ski turns are highly dynamic actions during which the direction of the skis and the body posture constantly change. In my experience, some people have difficulty in figuring out how to counter rotate the shoulders and when to start doing it. I can offer two instructions that can help with this. The first instruction is oriented toward skiers who have just started practicing step 1. And once the skier has learned to counter-rotate the shoulders at right time, the second instruction will help the skier to improve the performance of this step to make it more effective.

<u>*The first instruction*</u> focuses the skier on the angle between their shoulders and the skis. After passing the apex of the arc, the skis start to build an angle with the fall-line. The lower legs follow the skis because they are fixed in the boots attached to the skis. There is a natural desire to allow the torso to simply stay aligned with the legs too, so that the directions faced by the shoulders and skis are the same. The skier's task is to resist this natural torso alignment with the legs, by actively rotating the shoulders away from the direction of the skis. This motion will gradually build a larger and larger angle between the shoulders and the skis such that by the end of the arc, the line of the two shoulders becomes almost parallel to the skis below! This resistive counter rotation of the shoulders will cause the torsion.

Focusing on resisting the tendency of the upper body to follow the skis and lower legs was helpful for me when I began practicing the first step. For some other people though, a reformulated version of this instruction may be more helpful: when the skis start to rotate away from the fall-line, rotate the shoulders in the opposite direction. While the need to perform the counter rotation of the upper and lower body has been recognized by some instructors, we need to clearly understand when and why we do it. We do it during the second half of the arc to generate the body torsion that we will then release to pivot the skis in step 2.

Whether we think of it as resisting the natural tendency to follow the skis or as a counter-rotation, both prompt us to focus our attention on the angle between our shoulders and skis. This is quite different from focusing attention on the position of our shoulders with respect to the slope, which the traditional instruction to keep the shoulders facing downhill suggests us to do (I am not even mentioning the instruction to keep the torso "motionless", which makes sense for the observer only, not for the performer or the instruction to keep the torso "separated from the lower body", which does not make sense for anybody). To assess the relative position of the various rotations between our upper and lower body, we use the feeling of tension within our body caused by proprioception (sensory receptors located within our muscles and joints). In contrast, to keep the shoulders facing downhill, we would need to use visual information about the fall-line and our position with respect to it. Compared with proprioceptive sensing, processing visual information is 5-10 times slower. Also, processing visual information takes more cognitive recourses, thus diverting our attention from other aspects of skiing. Furthermore, it is often not easy even to determine the direction of the fall-line accurately, because it is constantly changing, depending on the terrain and moguls. These reasons make it difficult to follow the traditional instruction. I was never able to "keep facing downhill" as much as I tried to do so, while it took me minutes to learn to track the emergence of the angle between my lower and upper body by relying on the proprioceptive feeling of tension within my body. After you become familiar with this feeling (which should happen after a few correct turns), it will mean that you are ready to initiate step 2. Do not move on to practicing step 2 until you have obtained that feeling of tension caused by the body torsion.

The second instruction that helps us to create body torsion is better suited for more advanced skiers. While the first instruction is reactive (we react to ski rotation by resisting motion of the torso in the same direction), the second instruction is proactive. It suggests that instead of focusing on rotation of the skis and reacting to it with counter-rotation of the shoulders, we initiate each turn with an energetic slanted shoulder rotation (slanted shoulder motion that smoothly transits to shoulder rotation). This quick and forceful shoulder movement will cause our torso to bounce against the hips at the end of the shoulder rotation. If we time the rebound of the upper body from the lower body with the movement of throwing our pelvis forward to break the skis from the snow (step 2), we will add energy to the released skis, and they will transit to the other side of our body more swiftly.

Step 2. Pushing the body's weight forward. Once the torsion has been fully accumulated by the end of an arc, you are ready to perform step 2, i.e., to shift the body's weight forward. In this motion, you shift the pelvis towards the tip of the lower (outer) ski *by extending the knees, hips, and even the ankles* to the extent allowed by the boots. Since we extend the legs, our feet lag behind. Some people therefore feel this movement as *pushing the feet backward*. Although that feeling may help some skiers to guide the movement, the feet nevertheless keep moving forward across the snow together with the sliding skis, and they lag backwards only with respect to our own upper body. It is up to the reader to decide which instruction they like better, to push the pelvis forward or the feet backward. In both cases, the skier's weight will shift towards the skis and cross them over, which will eliminate ski edging. This weight shift will also reduce friction between the ground and especially the back portion of the skis. As a result, the body torsion will release and untwist the body. This body movement will pivot the skis around the front tips and transit them to the next arc.

Note that the use of the body torsion for pivoting the skis under the body can be effective only if the skier moves the body forward as a whole. A typical mistake here is that the skier just bends the torso forward at the hips. Crouching protrudes the head forward but the body weight itself does not shift forward enough, and the reduction in friction of the back portion of the skis with the snow will be insufficient for a good transition to the next arc. As I mentioned at the end of Chapter II, crouching is bad for step 1 as well because it is impossible to generate good torsion while bending the torso forward.

Step 2 is the phase where an instructor could help. Ask the instructor to go through sharp arcs on a mild slope, making deep turns in such a manner that he almost stops at the end of each arc. The energetic shift of the body forward is very noticeable during this type of skiing. Follow the instructor and mimic their movements. This helps to catch the moment at which one needs to push the body forward.

Leaning forward. There is a natural tendency to get in the "back seat" during skiing. The importance of preventing this cannot be overestimated. Leaning forward is one of the major instructions given by ski instructors. However, they do not explain when and how we should lean forward. I believe we perform two actions during each turn to keep the body leaning forward. I will refer to these actions as "*pushing the body weight forward*" that I have discussed in relation to step 2, and I will now introduce a new "body forward" command: "*weighting on the shins*". As we already know, pushing the body weight forward is performed in step 2. During this action, *we shift the body weight forward while extending the knees and hips*.

Figure 14. Weighing on the shins. The skier leans forward while carving through the arc by weighing on his shins with the entire body mass, as is emphasized by the red arrow.

This action however by itself is not sufficient, and so I wish to describe a second follow-up action, weighting on the shins, which is also necessary. We perform it when we finish step 2 and enter the next arc. This moment is demonstrated in Figure 10 by posture 4 and in Figure 11 by posture 5. In step 2, we have shifted our body's weight towards the front part of the skis and then after the "flying" transition, we land on the entire skis. This causes a natural tendency to land in the back-seat posture. We need to resist this tendency by shifting our weight forward. At this phase, *we shift our weight forward while flexing our hips and knees*. We also bend the ankles inside the boots until our shins start to press firmly against the tongues of the boots. We increase this pressure by leaning on the shins with our body mass through the flexed knees and hips, as the skier in Figure 14 does. It is important not to crouch during this phase. If we do this, our buttocks will jut out backwards, and the body weight will not be in the forward position.

Weighing on the shins does not move the body weight all the way to the balls of the feet. The body weight stays closer to the middle of the foot. This is necessary because if we keep the body weight too way forward during the second half of the arc, the back portions of the skis will be unloaded, and the shoulder rotation that we perform during this movement phase will pivot the skis around the tips too early, before we have finished the arc and accumulated good torsion. Thus, weighing on the shins allows us to load the skis along their length about evenly, and thus provide stability during torsion generation. Also, if we do not weigh on the shins, we will approach the end of step 1, where we have finished torsion generation, in the back seat. Pulling the body out of the back seat in step 2 will then take extra time and effort. In contrast, if we are weighing on the shins while going through the arc, it will be easy to initiate step 2 because only a small shift forward through extension of the legs would be sufficient to break the back portion of the skis free from the snow.

Even knowing that we need to perform these two actions, *leaning forward is still easier said than done*. At the beginning of each arc, the difficulty is in overcoming the natural tendency to sit back after landing on our skis. At the end of the arc, we need to throw our pelvis downhill by extending the legs. Psychologically, this can be very difficult to do, especially on a steep slope where this movement can feel like diving into a chasm. Leaning forward is therefore one of the most challenging components of skiing.

Using poles. A question that we have not yet touched on is: What do we do with the poles? It is best to start practicing the two steps without the poles. Position the arms wide and forward, at the chest level, in a semi-circular way, as the skier in Figure 15 does. Keep the arms in this position and practice making turns with the two steps. When the performance of the two steps becomes fluent and consistent, start using the poles. The arms should be in the same position as when you practiced without the poles. Their motion should be minimal. To plant the pole, swing it mainly by inclining the wrist, with little motion of the arm.

Figure 15. Positioning of the arms. In the frame A, the skier has just passed the apex of the arc, and he is starting to generate the body torsion. In the frame B, the skier has just initiated step 2. The skier keeps the arms in the same semi-circular position throughout the turn. He moves the poles largely by rotating the wrists, with very small swing of the arms.

How do poles help skiing? Some instructors suggest that keeping our arms in front of the body helps to lean forward. I doubt this because the arms stay in front of the body throughout the entire turn, and this does not decrease the tendency to land in the back seat at the beginning of each arc. However, planting the pole may help push the body forward in step 2, especially if we have a clear target for the pole in front of us, such as the tip of the next mogul that we want to go around. By reaching to plant the pole we are helping ourselves to push the entire body forward.

Other instructors suggest that planting the pole generates force that helps us to make a turn. The mechanical model of skiing that underlies the two-step technique does not include any significant effect of forces generated by the planted pole. The poles definitely do not play any important role in step 1. As I have just mentioned, planting the pole may help you shift the body weight forward in step 2.

Motor control research suggests another possible role of pole planting: it may help us to monitor our performance of step 2. Note that we plant the pole soon after initiating step 2 and we keep it planted while the skis are pivoting under the body. The grip of the skis with the snow is minimal at this phase of the turn, and therefore, we do not feel the position of our body with respect to the ground as strongly as during the other phases. The planted pole and the movement of the arm holding it gives us a reference about the movement of our body in space. This improves our ability to control our "flying" above the ground and helps us prepare for landing.

III.4. Skiing in Special Conditions

I figured out the two-step technique and started to practice it when I was in my mid-fifties. Now, in my sixties, I love skiing in conditions that I could not handle previously. Still, I realize that even though I am using the right technique, my skill will always remain limited. My favorite slopes are groomed black diamonds and blue bumps. I also enjoy skiing in a few inches of fresh powder. However, I do not think I will ever be able to ski fluently in especially difficult conditions, such as double-diamond slopes, big moguls, and knee-deep powder. While I believe that this limitation is caused by my age, it is possible that my comments below on how to ski in difficult conditions are not complete. Nevertheless, the two-step technique is still used even in these terrains, and I have rigorously tested the technique at lower levels of terrain difficulty. I therefore believe the recommendations provided next will help skiers to navigate difficult terrain.

Skiing on steep slopes. There are two major difficulties that emerge on steep slopes. The first difficulty is psychological. To perform step 2, *we need to push the pelvis downhill. This can be a scary thing to do*, especially if the steep slope is long, and we see that the bottom is far away. This fear disappears when we improve our skiing technique. Moreover, my own experience shows that when we progress in using the two-step technique, we start to perceive the same slopes as less steep than they looked to us previously.

The second difficulty that emerges on steep slopes is that we move faster due to the stronger effect of gravity. It is therefore *more difficult to keep our speed under control*. Still, we can keep our speed at any level we want. To reduce speed, increase the body torsion at the end of step 1. This will make the arcs sharper so that at the end of each arc, the skis are sliding forwards almost perpendicular to the fall-line. Moving more across and less down the hill by itself reduces the speed. In addition, when the skis are almost perpendicular to the fall-line and are edged, we can partially compensate for the gravitational force by pushing the skis against the ground to generate reaction force in the uphill direction. Interestingly, we can turn this relentless force of gravity into an aid when we perform step 2. Instead of shifting the body weight downhill with our muscles (by extending our legs), we can more easily allow the steep downwards gravitational force to itself pull our body weight over the skis. As when we actively perform step 2, this more passive allowance of gravity to do the work for us will still cause the release of the back portions of the skis from the snow, and the skis will again be freed up to easily pivot around the tips. Note that we can do this trick only on steep slopes, as the gravitational force that pulls us downhill needs to be steep enough.

Skiing moguls. The two-step technique used to ski on even terrain is also used to ski moguls. There are two ways to ski moguls, to initiate each turn on the mogul's top and slide down from it, or to go around the moguls. The first way can be used on mild moguls. High and steep moguls require going around them. Whichever way we use, it is only a matter of how we initiate each arc. In terms of the technique, there is almost no difference between the two ways. When we go around the mogul, we accumulate the body torsion while going along the arc circumventing the mogul. The arc ends under the mogul. Here, *the torsion allows us to slow down by using the back side of the next mogul below us as a break*. At the end of turning around the mogul, the skis are nearly perpendicular to the fall line. The body rotation and skip position allows us to very firmly press the ski bases against the uphill face of the next mogul, and by this way, to resist gravitational force and cancel it partially. This bouncing of the skis against the lower mogul is why big moguls become cut at their downhill side. Like on steep slopes, we can then use gravitational force to help us perform step 2, i.e. allowing it help pull our body weight down the steep slope over the skis, and thus, initiating the next arc around the following mogul.

When moguls are not steep, and we can slide down from them, using the back side of the bumps as breaks may not be necessary. Whether we slide down or go around a mogul, the tendency to get in the back seat is stronger than on even terrain. Therefore, the body weight needs to be pushed forward even more rigorously in step 2. Exaggerated planting of the poles ahead of us helps to push the body weight forward.

Skiing in deep snow. I may not have much experience in skiing in deep snow, whether it is powder or slash, but I know one thing for sure: the upper body leads our skiing movements, and the legs just follow. This is especially true for deep snow that resists leg movements more than packed snow. The following exercise done in 2-4 inches of fresh snow will allow you to experience the powerful effect of the upper body motion on the legs and skis. Shift the body weight back and start to rotate the shoulders side to side rhythmically. Relax your legs to let them give in to the effect of the upper body movements. You will see that each shoulder rotation will cause the skis to plow through deep snow in the opposite direction, with no effort from the legs.

My guidelines for skiing in deep snow is that *we again use the two-step technique although with a modification.* The first step remains the same as on packed snow – we generate the body torsion through a slanted shoulder rotation. We may however not lean forward as much as on groomed snow, and not weigh on the shins. During the second step, instead of shifting the body weight forward, which allows the skis to pivot around their tips, we shift the weight backward. As a result, the front parts of the skis will release their grip with the snow, and the skis will pivot around the tails.

Although this description of skiing in deep snow differs from what the expert skiers recommend doing, I believe that we are describing the same skiing approach in different words. For example, here are the instructions for skiing in deep snow given by Ron LeMaster in his book "Ultimate Skiing" (LeMaster 2009): "Keep your shoulders forward and your fore-aft balance around the middle of your feet. Roll forward to the balls of your feet going into the turn and, as you approach the bottom of your turn, move your feet forward a bit in anticipation of your skis slowing down as they go deeper into the snow." In the language of the two-step technique, "keep your shoulders forward" means "rotate the shoulders to generate torsion in the body", which automatically keeps your shoulders forward (see Section III.1). "As you approach the bottom of the turn": I described this as the end of the arc, the moment when we have accumulated torsion and are ready to initiate step 2. "…move your feet forward" can be read as "shift your body weight backward", which is step 2. Thus, we seem to be describing the same technique but my emphasis on the leading role of the upper body that is responsible for generation of torsion, and thus, of energy used to make turns, brings more clarity to this technique and the mechanical forces underlying it.

III.5. Drills

I have found two drills to be helpful when I teach the two-step technique.

The goal of *the first drill* is to allow the skier to feel how the upper body influences the motion of the skis. It is performed on a very mild slope so that the skier would not be frightened to ski straight down the slope. The skier should *point the skis down the fall-line, slightly bend the knees, and start to rotate the shoulders side to side*. While rotating the shoulders, the skier should try to relax the legs, so they will not resist the forces that the shoulder rotations exert on them. The skis will start to go through consecutive arcs, turning in the directions opposite to the directions of the shoulder rotations. This drill is a good way to demonstrate to the skier that the skis can turn with no action of the legs, just through the rotation of our shoulders.

The second drill helps skiers to learn how to generate torsion in the body. It is often a difficult element of the technique to learn because when we rotate the shoulders, we tend to allow the lower body to align with the shoulders. Then no torsion is generated. The second drill helps with learning how to resist this aligning. Figure 16 shows me demonstrating this drill. As you see in the left frame, we take both poles in both hands, holding both poles near their tops in one hand and near their ends in the other hand. The arms are positioned in the semicircle in front of the body, as we do when skiing. Then we slightly bend the knees and start to traverse the slope. Next, *we rotate the shoulders until the poles become almost parallel with the skis* (as you can see in the right frame of Figure 16). When rotating the shoulders, it is important to *keep the arms fixed in the semicircular position*. People often try to align the poles with the skis by rotating the arms in the shoulder sockets. That is incorrect. No motion at the shoulders or elbows should be performed.

The alignment of the poles with the skis is a clear visual cue informing us that the upper body has been rotated with respect to the lower body, and thus, torsion has been generated. Stay in this position for a while to feel the torsion and how the upper body is twisted with respect to the lower body. When ready, push the pelvis downhill. This will release the ski tails from the snow, and the skis will pivot around their tips and move to the other side of the body. Repeat while traversing the slope in the other direction. Although this drill does not include pulling the outer shoulder down, it allows us to feel how we achieve the counter rotation and verify it by checking whether the poles are parallel to the skis right before we initiate step 2.

Figure 16. **The second drill.** During the second drill, we hold both poles horizontally. The arms are firmly kept in the semicircular position in front of the body through the entire drill. We bend the knees and traverse the slope. At the beginning of the traverse, we hold the poles perpendicular to the skis, as shown in the left frame. Then we rotate the upper torso until the poles become almost parallel to the skis, as shown in the right frame. This motion creates torsion within the body. The skier in the right frame is ready for the next step: releasing the torsion energy by shifting the body weight forward. This will cause the skis to pivot around their tips and make a turn.

Conclusions

I came up with the two-step technique using my "leading joint" theory of control of multi-joint movements. Thus, the technique has a theoretical background. However, I have obtained substantial practical support for this technique. First, I used this technique myself, and my skiing dramatically improved. I have thoroughly tested the different elements of the two-step technique presented in this book. Second, I have used the two-step technique to teach quite a number of skiers. If the skier is physically fit and coordinated, and has skied for a year or more, they usually improve their technique very quickly, after 2-3 runs under my supervision. On average, I need 1-2 hours to teach a skier to ski right on mild slopes. After that, the skier can keep practicing the technique, gradually increasing the slope steepness. Comments on the 1-st edition of this book show that people easily get the two-step technique from reading the book, without my personal comments.

My experience as an instructor provides a strong support for the two-step technique as the most effective interpretation of downhill skiing that makes learning and teaching downhill skiing simple. However, I would not be surprised if some elements of the technique can be improved. I hope this book will inspire skiers with diverse skill levels to test this simple and transparent technique and comment on it. Please, leave a comment on Amazon. You can also email me to: effortless.skiing@gmail.com.

References

Dounskaia N (2010) Control of human limb movements: The leading joint hypothesis and its practical applications. Exercise and Sport Sciences Reviews, 4: 201-208.

Harb HR. Essentials of skiing. Hatherleigh Press, 2006.

LeMaster R. Ultimate Skiing. Muster the techniques of great skiing. 2009, p.197.

Printed in Great Britain
by Amazon